THE INTERNET IS IN THE RICE

THE INTERNET IS IN THE RICE

Poems

FOLUSHO ASUKWO

Folusho Asukwo

COVER AND ILLUSTRATION BY
SHIBLI NUNANI

CONTENTS

CHAPTER 1

Ojukokoro (Greed)

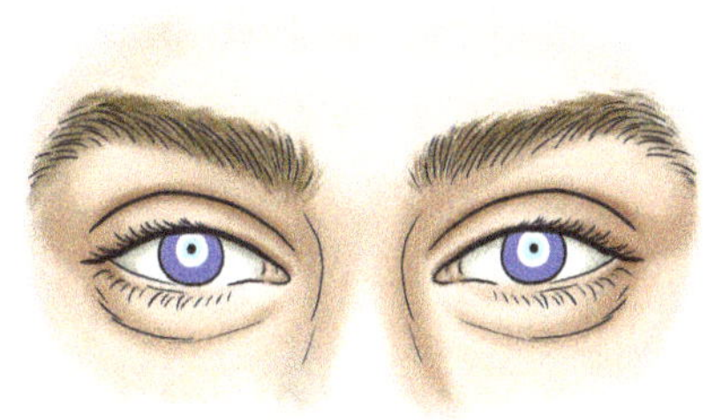

Alafia to Wahala

At long last

i've yearned to break fast from day

through grass onto a beach

i've treaded land now to wet my feet

dealt a blow from a crass wave

majestically an opposing force

I am fishing

for this is my enclave

you see my forefathers

my forefathers were brave

kept ships at bay and stalled bane

I am a warrior in the eyes of fish that swim deep

a lover of war

a warrior of peace

a compass led them to us

not one of moral fiber

as they arn't led by a chief

into the distance i gaze

a threatening fog symbolizes musket powder

a man clutching a book in his right hand

this man , a thief

it was on this day we lost our names

it was this day that sealed our fates

The formula for imperialism

Skip around and figure out what matches your vibe

Flip around and attempt to read the burnt scribes

decode the meaning between the scorches

then run around and hide them in a fortress

bury them in the ground and pass off the torches

and pose a conundrum as the culprit

Ancestral memory

Set a sail to the deep blue

with wooden tombs and chains too

babble in tongues so chic

so soft , the comfort captives

yet not your textbook romance languages

because they dare to scream "free me"

they speak Yoruba ,Fulani , Gan and Twi

learned massas language to say "fuck white hegemony "

they speak beauty and treaty

they speak freely

sing and dance for the world to listen

top deck for exercise

chanting but petrified , to ears that hear prey

praying you hear them

with a chain on everything but thier toungues

enchanting you with wild vernacular and love

with a chain on everything but thier toungues

enchanting you with wild vernacular and love

Slander dagger

Bring death to antiquated fodder

hold thier tongues in captivity with a hand bitter from a loosing fight

let it swim and struggle against the thick consistency of nectar that should be sweet

give them a taste of your plight

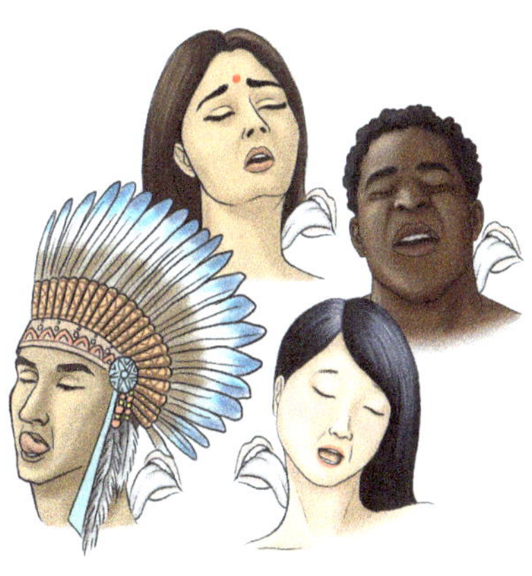

One light stand

Guns are masulince you would say right

a weapon with a potruding appendage

sending the message that the motive is to fuck lives up

The Nolympics

Black man

wrong to stand

threatened by the law

a weapon by default

loving is my heart

stoic is my persona

they say my fight is futile the oppression is over

oh but black man is a fast nigger

in a pool of blood his cup runneth over

to spill on the city streets

the same ones they claim to "clean up"

see from the hood to the favelas

these slave trained feet run so desperate just to find that the gun sounds at the finish line

blood in the cracks of the gravel while the gavel remains suspended the law perhaps reminiscing on black bodies suspended

knowing lady justice is blind but not deaf

knowing she heard a thud but not your hammer

only the cries of the disempowered

The dream of MMK
(massas master key)

The key to the door you bastard

you know what i'm talking about

not everybody has the same acess

don't tell me what I know

you sashe in the wind with it tied under a bow

spouting your false egalitarian rhetoric when you know

the truth is the keys we possess opens a trap door as we walk through

trap doors like red lines

trap doors like court fines

trap doors like "all lives"

we fall through

Anarchy

We have to see anarchy for wickedness to take form

for hate to be purged in the open

to see you and you are broken and would take human tears as a token of power

In the age of aquarius

The big lie

Through the better part of the week you groan in cadence at the sound of your alarm clock

at the third tap realizing you have 10 minutes to brush your teeth and 5 to iron your jump suit for the day

your coperate overlords are waiting

waiting for you to tuck yourself into a cubical bespoke to your woes with the perk of hiding your side profile

a deep sigh as you anticipate the sporadic summons of a pedantic superior

an inhale that denotes the smell of aged carpets

the rent is due

you are chasing tailwinds to make headway

running parallell to your misery

swallowing a scream that only dares to leak as you road rage home

certain you went through the contract with a fine toothed comb

in disbelief of the lie they sold you

Certain you're trapped

Me Three

Tables turn on those who refuse to have a seat at the head

with thier navals pressed at the edge

the cloth don't shift ,the marbles are steady

I declare this a place with the marbles together

I declare this a place of sanity

and we bring ruin on anybody who dares to take the cloth off

they are nasty we eat here

we only grope privates under and dangle a chandalier of stars over

reach while we feast on the succulence of your thigh

reach and a chair will draw to catch your fall

just mind your manners and remember

the rules are for me to speak and your mouth to only open

are you ready to please me

are you ready to be great

In the age of aquarius

Welcome to the world wide web

check in for validation

check in for news

and just check in

check in

check out of the moment

check out of the elation of connection

and capture the moment

tell them the camera is on

the world is watching

and watch them attempt to prove they are amongst the living

hashtag lit, hashtag my best life

fall into despair behind a screen that reflects a face dripping with sweat

Stumble over unlaced boots not fit for the treadmill you want to keep up with

stumble and chew on a curated digital footprint that fills you with envy

you see i myself on somedays are a molded caricature of who you wish to be

omitting my despressive state with a look of happy

because the people deserve it

the world is watching

Initiation

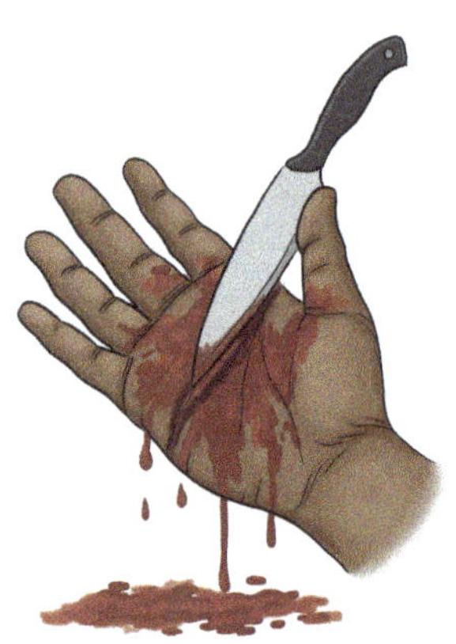

"I am a man with hemophilia sworn into a toxic society by the cut of a hand"

Poison tear drops

The water is on the horizon

so much of it is welling up

it's on the horizon

i hold myself back from pouring up

a glass of pain drink and hope you vomit

or die and shoot across the sky like a comet

I might make a wish or the waters may rise again

foreign waters you could never conprehend

Leap

With my eyes closed I explore the void

my feet carry me as my vessel pierces the unknown

brushing duality I come in my own

as I pine for the throne i face adversity

they mistaken my blindness for hubris

they look at me

Odontophilia

Wear your face out

it's wicked out today

it's wicked out everyday

they long to hunt your smile

all while begging you to show them

so give them a crack to satisfy thier fix

Snorkel to atlantis

I dive into uncertainty

driven by the pursuit of freedom

the shackles are hefty

do I drown below or find the kingdom

leave me to my demons

they've labored for thier supper

chasing me since I was in the womb of my mother

where the light does not reach the darkness swallows

the disdain for peace in my heart follows

Ploy Scouts

The eyes are cold

They see   they saw   they know

observe the weak

the meek   the dark the bold

up in the sky

the stars they crash   they burn

the eyes

they tear up at smoke

unaware of thier projection now they are woke

" My pain was clandestine in thier midst , so I destroyed all tangible merits to break the facade "

A cinematic performance

And if pebbles indeed skip lakes

do boulders galavant the ocean

do my hands wield the strength

the proposition morphed my posture into a militant stride

the boy rolling the curtains said " here he comes I hope you're ready "

the silence broken by an accusatory monologue

telling the audience a story for which i hoped ears were keen

the room sovereign to the echo of my voice , bearing the grudge of a bastards cry

you see I could be better , or I could be wiser

the grio has shattered my compass with stories of dark beasts that prevailed

lived to tell the tale wagging thier tails

hungry for more

asking for something to chase

fear to feed

to be loving , to be kind was the most seductive bait

and to be hated would be fine if they couldn't catch me

what lives in me now is ugly

a bastards cry

a cinematic performance

" False pride finds i'ts conviction in humiliation "

A blur

I put my wine bottles outside my room one at a time

maybe that throws off the fact that i'm a junior alcoholic

"junior" the prefix I use to minimize judgement

empty they are because they filled me with giggles and a blur

false happiness

a blur

the kind you only see through the eye of a liquor bottle

I stand in the fire

I stand in the fire

conflicting with the desire of those who conspire

I stand in the fire

ridiculed or admired

but never call me a liar

I stand in the fire

I wear protective attire

don't call me a martyr

niether am I a fireman

I nuture the flame

ammunition to shame

i'm not a martyr

Renegade

If the cult wants me to bow

then the trumpets have to make a sound

the fat lady has to sing

children have to gasp from her inhale

it is a song worth singing

frost from hot breath

making us to dance in the rain

a rhythm from the Gods

I move on that accord

all in favor of denying shackles of the mind

all aboard to make the tyrants cry

a song worth hearing

the interlude a question worth asking

what is reality they say

it's a zeitgeist captured in a moving painting

a dystopia of our design

a figment of our imagination

the illusion of identity bending the corners of pages yet to be turned

your every move inevitably telling a story

but us, only getting a glimpse of this page

told to sit still

since obedience is reverence

and a holy word dousted in sacrilage makes the world spin

listen

open your ears

for a command

for direction

for permission

Vaultage

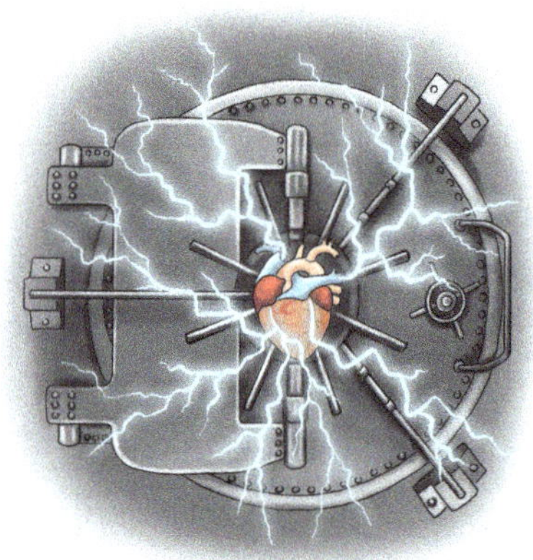

Origami

No i'm not good on paper

but paper for me was always a blank canvas

paper for me was meant to be folded up and made to fly

like a jet with cockpit

while darting eyes follow and judgement vomits

waiting for the ink to dry from the breeze

waiting ...

for mercy

A net worth vetting

In bed with a voice that sais

"lets focus on us "

lonliness is just deceit that forces you to open up

to put your heart on the line

the longest ever waited on

the deepest feeling anticipated

questioning "should i wait for the conversation to be initiated ? "

stepping into a place of tender loving care

how pleasing to the ears

long term you say

but short term we play

play in fear like Saw

play in fear

in fear of rejection , dodging unrequited love

while loving those who reject us because they make us feel safe

they make us feel safe by giving us the answer up front

Binoculars

Ever wanted to be looked at like somebody

like something

have you ever wanted to run to a place where no one knows your name so they can call you "face"

Trip of faith

I'm trying to find my landing

when i find myself tripping over my words

trying to express myself to you

for you are so important

maybe it's the oxytocin that rushes my mental when you are present

maybe it's how your eyes smile at my presence

i'ts hard for me to look at you and focus on my message

do you trust me when i say " i love you " looking down

Treasurer

Hold your heart out

in the palm of your hands

so i may examine it throb

in the atmossphere the pulsing echoes out into the universe

i cry when i see your blood go to waste

a collective disgrace

i smile as a friendly face to close the space .... and sanity is lost

Butter finger

I wish my fingers wouldn't sweat so much when i explore the curvature of your body

i wish they could weave hand signs that spell your initials

leave indelible prints proclaimed by you to be the key to your heart

but right now i'll settle to have you wrapped around my finger so i can

love you ofcourse

House of scorpio

Bodies gyrating

The sounds of moaning hugging my ears

And I reach for your face to feel that you see me

Reaching climax but delaying the gratification

and the impact of loins drown the background of moaning

Breath condensing and melding with sweat

If neither of us is to pass out then what is sex

Our shadows dancing

putting grafitti to shame

The bed squeaking

Eyes twitching

Legs shaking

the head board keeping score

Grafitti

Your will is weak

you've oozed your life force out onto a masterpiece of a canvas

gasping to catch your breath

just to follow it with words you don't mean

Ingo swan

It was from a fortress underground I looked at you

sketching your surroundings

finding solitude to activate eyes

an ocular prowess peering beyond the walls you build

a defiance of physiscs

love ripping the jaws of space and time

my ears drawn by a vortex to hear your laughter from a distance

realising I was abused by admiration

the swiftness of a beautiful bondage held me captive

I was still for the love of dancing

sprinting to catch you but never panting

a slave to you

and even now , if you were to go

a pinch ,maybe a scar

*a tapping finger to join the others incapable of salvaging the crumbs of love
eroded*

your love an algedonic whirlwind

nostalgia that chases my shadow

a screenshot in my memory bank depicting the love of a lifetime

satisfaction

Securing the wrath

Manifest war to me

you beautiful creature

let me delight in your ugly

the passion in your hatred shows me you love me

The codependent

You're toxic just the way i like em

you give me stimuli in an otherwise bleak existence

cause me pain and make my heart dance with the pleasure you bring as restitution

nothing but a contribution to the attention I crave

Picture perfect

Picture perfect

we skin the surface

with little knowledge if they are worth it

"I had a savior complex. I would seek out people with wounds and try to heal them in hopes of vicariously living through thier recovery. The paradox of a selfish empath lived in me."

Balancing act

It is known to a degree

thinking in the heat can be hard

but it's in this smoldering ambiance that life spreads the cards

you are to think on your feet and stand on them

lay your hand on the spread

should you succumb to the growl of your gut over the persuasion of your head

CHAPTER 5

A skin graft for Manniquens

"

Morality is intangible to metric, but can be measured by gauging the disparity of brutality necessary to survive and the excess amount you willingly employ. "

Breath

The air feels like home

every sip of oxygen

the lucky day

a pitcher

a pitcher filled

a rage of thunder on a sunny day

calm you wish you were

strong lifts you up

you are pulsing with the rythym

the dilation of your alveoli

the expansion of your diaphragm

a motion

the subtle declaration that i am bold

you are wicked for you are man

at your lowest you personify wrath

but in balance you lead with a gentle sword cutting the wind

etched in the blade is a message to them saying

" I am breathing and expanding , we are love and with this sword , I free you

'" I dont expect you to belive me when i tell you who i am . After all , each of us were ushered into the darkness to find wonder that bred desire"

Blooming

Dust to dust

bones into ground

to orchestrate an apparatus that dosn't yeild to gravel

they put you in a box

your true nature unexposed

left dead quiet

with vines creeping to make strong roots

inching to give you life

redifining your purpose

the courage to reach you

the thirst of nature blossoming to a new day on your behalf

blooming only with the sun to shine and you as the seed

voiding opinion

Beyond scope

*sometimes my writing reveals my limits and compels me to resent the bandwidth
of my brain*

language fails me

sight blinds me

and touch fosters distance

I long to fill the gaps in language

like a munchkin makes a donut whole

evidence that I am a soul bathed in body and body padlocked with skin

evidence of more

Sonder Drive

Up a street you're not familiar with

could you lean away from the steering wheel

could you make me feel warm

like the slight rush you feel at the edge of a casino table

the first shot of the night

I want to live

give me a reason

I would be delighted if you could give me grand theft auto and a drive in movie

my head rested and my back pressed against the chair

aching to break the glass just to feel the wind in my hair

my head up to observe movement and i see it all

the trees , the signs , and the people

a translucent veil of sonder embraces my cornea to show me the people

and i'm warm now

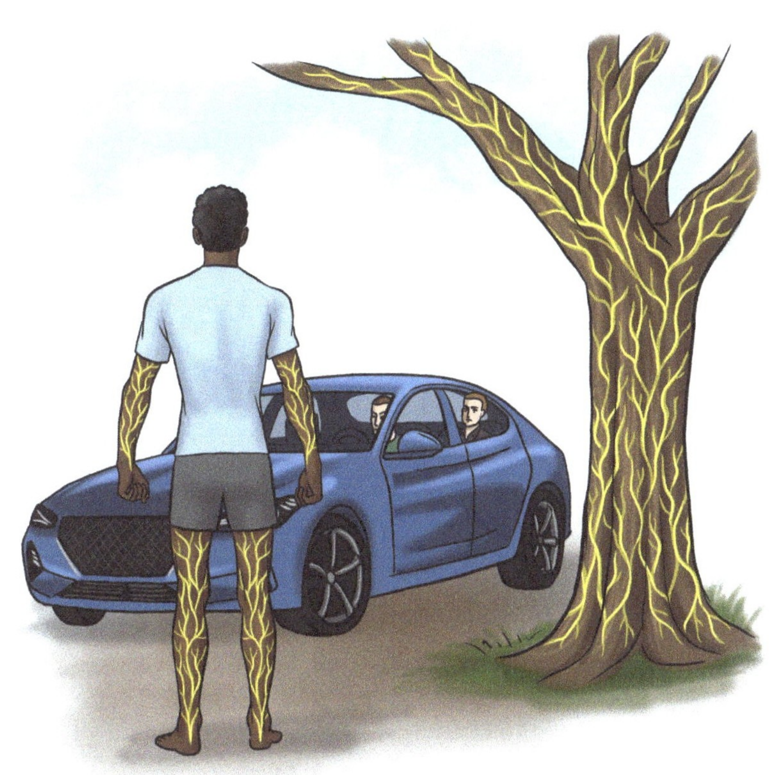

In the light

It was a windfall

a surge of serendipity

i felt welcome

embraced

I should remember a hug is not poison

a call to action

on guard

a knife to sharpen

a potion

the kind that compels your tongue to bow to your bottom jaw

there you are in awww

swept in a a dichotomy of emotion

like your knees bow to rythym and buckle in fear

the thrill of uncertinty

the slap of an angel

the death of who you wanted to be

because imposter syndrome can't shake you